ROOM TO BE PEOPLE

Room to Be People

An Interpretation of the Message
of the Bible for Today's World

JOSÉ MÍGUEZ BONINO

Translated by Vickie Leach

FORTRESS PRESS   PHILADELPHIA

Library of Congress Cataloging in Publication Data

Míguez Bonino, José.
　　Room to be people.

　　Translation of Espacio para ser hombres.
　　1.　Theology—Addresses, essays, lectures.
　　I.　Title.
　　BR85.M48513　1979　　　230　　　78-14662
　　ISBN　0–8006–1349–X

7398K79　Printed in the United States of America　1–1349

CONTENTS

23   1530

PREFACE

The chapters in this book are the fruit of a discussion series held in the church hall of a Protestant congregation in Buenos Aires. Both those who call themselves Christians and those who do not took part in the conversations. Their purpose was to shed light on the real meaning of the Christian faith—not to provide definitive answers to compelling questions, but rather to provoke serious reflection on issues important to everyone. The participants, like you perhaps, were simply and sincerely searching for glimpses of truth.

After I gave a brief presentation on a theme, the participants divided into small groups that discussed the theme and delved into questions that came up; the groups then reunited and discussed the theme in common. The result was a shared understanding.

This written presentation follows the format of those meetings. I have not revised what was said, except for some obvious corrections of grammatical errors which naturally arise in any spontaneous presentation. Please excuse any repetition or inexactness of expression which is also inherent in such an adaptation from oral discussion. My aim is faithfulness to the original flow of spontaneous ideas.

What I am offering you then is not an individual treatise, but rather the result of a living dialogue. I do it in the hope that it will invite you too to participate in and explore more deeply the themes that are presented.

The open character of this presentation is not merely a literary device. I believe it corresponds to the core themes of the book: God, his purpose, plan, and action; and people, their faith, hope, and response. No one, after all, is an authority on these themes. There are no scholars of the great mysteries. There are only seekers. And the only thing a seeker can do is share with others the results of the search, and invite them to join in continuing it.

Moreover, since the Christian faith is based on the free action of God, the Christian is like a beggar who says to another beggar, "Let's go together. I know where they will give us bread." This is exactly what is intended here.

This means something very important for you. God and the Christ and the Christian faith are not simply themes to be passively received. Of course, it is possible to study and objectively evaluate Christian truths without committing yourself to them. But that is just information. What is needed is transformation—the kind of understanding that penetrates beyond facts to reality, the kind of understanding that can change lives.

And so the theme of God can only be communicated passionately, as a vital reality which gives meaning to our lives, and it can only be received passionately (which does nòt mean blindly or without reflection), as a clarion call which demands a response. It is in this sense that this passionate encounter—this struggle to see God more clearly, which words alone cannot produce but which happens through grace—binds your entire life, not to mere religious observance but to God's own plan to create a whole world of kinship. That is the call. And that is the challenge.

1

ONLY AN ATHEIST CAN BE A GOOD CHRISTIAN

This curious title is not merely an attention-getting device. It came out of an exchange between the atheist philosopher Ernst Bloch, who had a profound interest in the influence of the biblical message on the history of hope, and the Christian theologian Jürgen Moltmann, who was trying to uncover the core of hope in biblical revelation. Bloch said, "Only an atheist can be a good Christian," to which Moltmann replied, "But only a Christian can be a good atheist." I have cited these statements because they sum up admirably the idea that I want to develop in this chapter.

Often we think that the most important thing is for someone to believe in God, to believe in his existence, to have faith. Some years ago, former president Dwight D. Eisenhower said that the most important thing is for a person to have faith; it doesn't matter in what, just that one believes. It is really common knowledge. And yet if we think for a moment we would understand that some of the most savage actions performed by human beings have been caused by the faith, the work of people who believed with all their hearts and were truly convinced that they were serving God.

Neither belief in God nor the strength of that faith constitutes any guarantee. In truth, the important thing is precisely in *which God* we believe, or the object of that faith. It is also significant that the early Christians were accused of being atheists and were judged and condemned as such for refusing to believe in the ruling gods of their society.

Why Are There Atheists?

In one sense, Bloch's statement is correct—only an atheist can be a good Christian. That is, only the person who denies certain "gods" can have faith in the real God. Therefore let us stop for a moment to consider atheism. Why is someone an atheist? What arguments do we give to someone who refuses to believe in God?

There are some who say, "I believe in science and therefore I can't accept the existence of God." Why should someone see science and God as mutually exclusive? The simple response is that religion has frequently presented God as a substitute for science, knowledge, and investigation. We are not only talking about cases of religious fanaticism in which the people replace science, for example, the use of medicine, with a superstitious faith, and believe that God performs miraculous or magic deeds. I am thinking rather of those who use God as the explanation for those things which have no scientific or rational explanation.

Look at history. Primitive humans had no explanations for a great number of things. They did not know how day followed night, for example. And they sought the explanation in the gods. There was a god of the day and light, and another of the night and darkness. The struggle between the two of them became the explanation for the succession of night and day. We know the many different stories of the gods—myths—that were used to explain meteorological phenomena (storms, eclipses, tides, and so forth). However, one fine day we learned that the movements of the earth and sun, the force of gravity or atmospheric electricity, would permit us to decipher these mysteries. And then God was in our way. History has repeated itself a thousand times. Yet there always remained a little space where God still could serve as the explanation: life, the human mind, energy. But science is slowly filling all these spaces, and God is displaced from the universe. A God-explanation which is really a substitute for science has little future in a universe dominated by human knowledge. From there it seems that there is no other road to follow than to become an atheist.

In this sense, one has to be an atheist in order to be a good Christian, because the Christian faith rejects this substitution. In the magnificently poetic story of creation at the beginning of the Bible, God gave humans the use of and dominion over creation. Using a meaningful expression of that time, God gave Adam the authority to name things, that is, to know them, to rule them, to manage them, to learn their secrets and be able to use them for his own purposes. In other words, God entrusts scientific and technological activity to people. The realization of this work is not a challenge to God, it doesn't reduce his space; it is rather collaborating with God in completing the duty which he has entrusted to us. Of course, there are questions that surround all scientific and technological activity, and the faith responds to these. What function does science have? What use does technology have? What plans or ends do they serve? But by no means does this mean that God is left in the still unexplained corners of the universe. Only for that God who is a substitute for human understanding are we Christians also atheists.

Others would tell us: "I don't believe in God because I believe in humanity." The more emphasis we place on human beings, they would insist, the less space there is for God. They are on either side of the scale: if one side goes up the other goes down, and vice versa. The religions, they tell us, sacrifice people to God. In order to recover the value of human beings, therefore, it is necessary to sacrifice God. We well know that some religions have often

sacrificed people to God, literally, in bloody human sacri-
fices. They taught that God required the sacrifice of human
beings as acknowledgment of his divine power.

It is not necessary to recount all the cultures that practiced human sacrifice. How many people think even today
that in order to honor God we have to deprive ourselves of
our humanity, of those values which make our life richer,
more pleasant, fuller, in a word, more human: love, joy,
culture, communion, and friendship. Whoever values these
things feels obligated to choose between humanity and
God, and often chooses the former.

This point of view is far from what the Bible really
teaches about God. Nevertheless it has predominated
throughout vast sectors of Christianity during many epochs.
This was one of the great struggles Jesus had with those who
made religion an end in itself and human beings its slave.
For example, God instituted a day of rest, for people to
pause in their work and enjoy the contemplation of the
world, the community of the family, the glory and communion with God himself. But this rest had become a prison:
they could not care for a sick person, or travel, or cut
an ear of wheat, or eat any grain. It was God's day and
therefore a day denied to people. And Jesus responded in-
dignantly: "You have things backwards—the day of rest
was made for man, and not the reverse" (paraphrase of
Mark 2:27). What better way can there be of honoring
God on that day than by giving health, joy, and fullness to
life! The religious leaders of Jesus' day wanted to honor
God by limiting and putting barriers on human life. But,
according to the true faith, to honor God means to give
freedom, to enrich life, to honor human beings. That is the
will of God.

Finally, others would tell us: "I don't believe in God
because he is an instrument of the exploitation and sub-
jugation of humankind." Once again we have to understand
that this has frequently been practiced and even now is the

case. The Brazilian educator Paulo Freire told of the dialogues he often had with the poor peasants of his country. The conversations centered around the peasants' situation: their misery, the fact that they could not own the land which they worked nor even the fruits of that land, the impossibility of meeting their minimal needs, let alone getting ahead. Finally they came to the conclusion that things were that way because they had always been that way. A person was a peasant because the parents had been peasants, and the grandparents, and the grandparents of the grandparents! Some people are born peasants, and others property owners: that's how things are. And to the question, "Why is it so?" the response of the peasant would be simply: "God made it that way." Think about what this means: if God made it that way, if God wants it that way, it is not necessary to change the situation. To try to change it would be to disobey the will of God. This argument has been repeated more than once by property owners and priests: "God has made rich and poor, property owners and peasants, and it is not necessary to change the order created by God." Whoever rebels against that order logically rebels against the God who has created and maintains it. If God guarantees the present state of things, in order to change it is necessary to reject God.

Once again, even a very superficial reading of the pages of the Bible would be enough to bring down that God. We will return to this theme later. But it is important to say from now on with all clarity that the God of the Bible in no way guarantees the exploiter his or her property, nor has God authorized the slavery of the oppressed. On the contrary, as one of the prophets has said, whoever sustains the order of things "does not know God." Furthermore the ruler who practices justice and protects the rights of the weak and the poor is the one who "knows God" (Jer. 22: 13–16).

When someone says, then, "I don't believe in God because I believe in humanity" or "I don't believe in God because I believe in justice," I must respond that I don't believe in that God either! Only a passionate atheist to those gods can be a true Christian. The one who adores a god who is a substitute for science, or who puts humans down, or who guarantees situations of injustice, has placed trust in false gods. The more faith that person has, the worse he or she will become, because such faith is directed at something other than God.

To Become a Believer, You Have to
Abandon the Gods

How is it possible for these aberrations to occur? Where do these false gods come from? The Bible frequently tells us that we invent gods, we make them up. Of course it is clear that we fabricate images of gods. The prophet Isaiah joked about people who took pieces of wood and carved them to make images of themselves. With the chips that were left over, Isaiah said, they could make a fire and pre- pare roasted meat. They placed on a pedestal the carving which they made from the same wood, knelt before it and prayed, "My God, save me." He ridiculed the adoration of images in that manner. But, more profoundly, Isaiah de- nounced all the mystification by which we fabricate ideas about God, concepts of God, in proportion to our con- veniences and interests. We invent gods to defend our selfish interests, to justify our guilty tranquility in the face of evil, to borrow the strength to fight for a better world, to justify our egos, our family class, and national pride. And then we adore them, when in truth we are adoring ourselves. For example, Jesus says that "You cannot serve God and mammon [the god of money or riches]" (Matt. 6:24c). And Paul says that "avarice is idolatry," (Col. 3:5) which means the adoration of a false god.

We certainly do not always realize what we are doing—

sometimes because we do not give it a religious character. We say that we are not religious, that we have no interest in religion, but in truth we have made certain things—wealth, power, comfort—into gods and we sacrifice everything to them. Or, what actually is even worse, we call ourselves Christians, we say that we adore the true God, that we believe in Jesus Christ, but we are in reality merely disguising our own selfish group and class interests under these facades. We have kept the name of God, but we have ripped out his substance. There can be no true faith unless these false gods are destroyed. This is the first problem: in order to believe in God, you have to disbelieve in the gods we have made. You have to begin to be an atheist regarding these gods.

God Is Not Alone

The struggle of the true God against the false gods is a recurring theme in the Bible. This obliges us to ask ourselves, "What is the true God?" or better still, "How is he?" or perhaps more precisely, "Who is he?" A daily paper in Buenos Aires ran a commentary about God the other day that ended with the ancient definition: "God is the one, he who is alone." Actually, this affirmation is just about the greatest heresy, the biggest lie that can be told about God. In terms of the Christian faith as it has been revealed in the Bible, as it was taught and lived by Jesus Christ, God is precisely the one who is *never* alone, the one who has never wanted to be alone. God is the one who decided to create the world and relate it to himself. He created human beings in order to make a society, in order to invite them to work together with himself in the transformation and perfection of all creation.

From the beginning God tells us: "Let's make this world together." God has laid the foundations, has given it a reality, a world like a garden to be worked, so that it bears fruit and becomes beautiful. He has created a human family to increase and form a community of work and love. When God invites, "Let's make this world together," people begin to cultivate the garden, to manage and rule the world, to name and discover the secret of life, and to become rich and useful. There is more in that same Bible story: each time we destroy this society—and we are constantly doing this—God repairs it and makes it over and gives it a new future and a new purpose.

The true God is not "the one who is alone." On the contrary, it is he who invites us to be with him. He is a God who is more concerned with others, with the world and people, than with himself. This is highly suggestive because we habitually think about a God who is out there, distant, taking care of those who think about him, are concerned with him, are trying to protect him, and satisfy him. The God of the Bible, on the other hand, is constantly busy in the world, in its course, in the creation of life and its fullness, in justice and truth among people. When he talks to us—which often occurs in the Bible—it is not to speak about himself, but rather about his purpose and his desire for the world, for us. In the Bible there are no discussions of the nature or the being of God. The topic of conversation between God and humankind is people themselves. Whoever is not interested in this does not have to talk to God. Because God is completely involved in his plan for the world, he invites men and women to think about this plan, to seriously consider it, and to join with him in realizing it.

The focal symbol of the Christian faith, the cross, is the strongest affirmation of God's decision to be with us. God has taken his involvement with human beings in the realization of this plan so seriously that he does not hesitate to risk his own participation in human life, in its poverty and frailty, even in death, in order to restore society to us. The God of the Bible is a God for others and for himself. He is a God who suffers, who plays, who takes risks in his plan for creating a world. When we mention Jesus Christ we are speaking of this, of a "bet" which God has made on human beings, offering himself as the guarantee. And he gave his life. It is right that those philosophers who imagined a god in their likeness—a kind of universal philosopher with their own thoughts, who dispassionately contemplated the world —should feel disoriented and perplexed. This Christian God "of flesh and in the flesh" as one Spanish intellectual once called him, this passionate God who allows himself to be beaten and insulted and crucified in order to seal his desire for the transformation of the world, only he is, in Christian terms, the true God.

Powerful but Not Tyrannical

Nevertheless some will say, "All this about God wanting to be with men and women, participating in the contingencies of history, taking risks, does this mean that God isn't powerful, that he isn't sovereign?" It would seem that such a God is not really God at all. But let us pause and ask ourselves: What does it mean to be sovereign? What does it mean to be powerful? As often happens, we define terms in our own way, which may be different from the way God himself has defined them, and then we attribute these qualities to him. Thus we have compared *powerful* and *sovereign* with our selfishness and inhumanity which pretend to be just that. Jesus himself once had to correct his disciples about this. "You know that those who are supposed to rule over the Gentiles lord it over them, and their great men exercise authority over them. But it shall not be so among you; but whoever would be great among you must be your servant, and whoever would be first among you must be slave of all. For the Son of man also came not to be served but to serve, and to give his life as a ransom for many" (Mark 10:42–45).

Here is a different concept of power. If we want to compare terms, think about the creative power of an artist who molds the clay over and over again, who constructs and reconstructs and revises it. Do not think about the magician whose magic wand touches things and they disappear. God is powerful, like the artisan who never tires or gets discouraged, but keeps on working with infinite patience and perseverance, who begins again as often as is necessary until what is created is what was intended, the plan. Such a one is powerful because he or she is faithful to the work, does not get bored or tired until the work is completed. Or let us think about the good rulers, not about the tyrants who subdue and dominate their people. The good rulers are those who encourage their people, guiding them in the search for their goals, showing them the way, enabling them to achieve their destiny. God is not a ruler who arbitrarily determines the way of his world or magically directs it from above; he is the sovereign who guides, encourages, accompanies his people. To believe, in Christian terms, means to enter society with that God in order to work with him. It is to sign a contract by which we pledge ourselves to participate in his plan for the world, to make that plan our own. It is important therefore to know which contract we signed, and with whom. Doing it with any of the gods we invented is not the same as doing it with the God whom the Bible reveals to us, the God who calls us to create with him a world that is worth living in.

THEMES FOR REFLECTION

Evil and Freedom

"If God is working in the world," commented one of the participants in our discussion, "he is doing very poorly, because, as we have already said, this world isn't working very well." This is an old dilemma—and an important one.

Many people have tried to answer it, trying to excuse God for the things that go wrong. The task of excusing God is necessary when the God-explanation or the arbitrary-sovereign-God of which we have spoken is employed. But things are different when we talk about the God who builds a society with human beings.

Let us first put it in terms of a simple and juvenile comparison. Sometimes after we give a child a little job, we will see the child wandering around, leaving the task unfinished or working on it "like a monkey"; then we feel the temptation to shout, "Go on out and leave it alone, I'll do it myself." Sometimes we give in to the temptation, even though we know that this only frustrates the child and hinders the learning process. If the comparison does not seem too childish to you, we could say that God never tells us: "Go on out, I'll do it myself." Instead he is constantly inviting us to begin again, because his purpose is not to make things but persons. And they can only be made in this way.

There is a fable about an angel who returns to earth and gets very upset because of the tragic errors and suffering of human beings. When he is once again in God's presence, he asks God why he does not intervene and solve people's problems. "Isn't there anything we can do?" And the answer comes back: "We have given them love and fire. We can't do anything else." This means that God has given us the security of his presence and his love, the forces necessary to build a human community and serve each other in love. He has given us the possibility of materially transforming and recreating the world. He will be with us until that love and fire create a new humanity. But he will not leave us all alone!

It is a very difficult procedure. But is there any other way humanity can be made? This is another old philosophical dilemma in reference to creation. When God made the world and men and women, were they not an emanation

of the divine? Are they not a "piece of God"? God created
something that is "other" than himself, distinct, autonomous.
It is then, in a certain sense, a limitation of himself, similar
in some way to having a child, in which case a free will and
freedom are born which are not subjected to our discretion,
which can only be guided through our prodding dialogue
and persuasion. God wanted persons who were not a part of
himself, but rather of others. And for that he provided the
world—the space given to men and women to be themselves. God will respond to their calls, take part in their
battles, suffer with them, and rejoice with them. But he
will not invade their space, he will not transform it into
something which he controls. This is the very core of the
Christian faith.

Jesus Christ did not come to substitute for people but
rather to open the way for them to realize their human plan.
When we say that God is all powerful, we do not mean that
he substitutes for us, or prevents the existence of evil with
a decree. And while he reserves the freedom to definitively
save his plan from failure, he still retains the capacity and
patience to continue working and to complete his plan—
that is our gift—throughout all the frustrations and suffering
of history. A noted Latin American theologian once said
that the whole gospel can be translated into one statement:
"No love is lost on this earth." That is the only guarantee.
For this reason God is all powerful.

Believers Who Do Not Believe

An ancient question and concern of Christians has been
to understand how some atheists can dedicate themselves to
a true love of their neighbor and a positive transformation
of the world. We will come back to this theme later. But for
now let us begin by noting two approaches to the problem.
One is to admit that we do not really know who are atheists.
It is clear that we should respect a person and not assign a

belief that he or she cannot accept. It is a form of Christian imperialism to say, "The good, whether they believe in Jesus or not, are the Christians." But at the same time, precisely because there are so many distortions of the faith, there are people who have not rejected the true God but rather the caricature of him as presented by us Christians. Their rejection is often rooted in a fidelity to the true God, although they do not realize it, and that is our fault, not theirs.

Surely it is in this sense that we ought to interpret the story of Jesus about the father who sends his sons to work in his vineyard. The older one answers, "Yes, father," but he does not go; the younger one refuses: "I'm not going," but then he goes anyway (Matt. 21:28ff.) The message is obvious. Which of the two behaved like a son? In the most literal terms, the true son is the one who perceives the will of his father, happily accepts it, and does it. But in a world in which religion has been empowered more than once by "the image of the Father" and has distorted it, at times an active human rebellion is more faithful than mere lip service, which really constitutes a rejection of duty.

However, this is not a question of the exaltation of rebellion and atheism as if they are always born out of a healthy rejection of false gods. They can also represent—and often do—a rejection of the true God. To enter into society with the true God is to risk a costly adventure. It is to take the risks that he has taken, even death. It is to accept the proposition of not simply living alone, for yourself, but rather of transforming the world through love and fire. And that often involves the sacrifice of your own comfort, security, self-esteem, status, and image. It includes recognizing your own mistakes and weaknesses and failures. It is not strange that we are bowled over by this calling, and that we try to save what is "ours." Sometimes we Christians do this by distorting God so that he does not demand so

much, and in this way we justify our own selfishness. Other
times we do it—like the atheists—by denying God's invitation to us. We say, "There is no God," and so we free
ourselves of this problem. Of course, this is deceitful. It is
as if I have convinced myself that there is no one before
whom I am held accountable—my family, society, the law
—I am actually responsible to no one. Reality will soon
awaken me from this fantasy. There is one kind of atheism
which we all possess to some degree: the rejection of God
in order to avoid commitment; killing God so that I do not
have to feel obligated for my neighbor, or to give less weight
or value to this responsibility. Then we employ all kinds of
philosophical arguments to support our rejection.

The Jealous God

Some people have been a little scandalized by the "intransigence" of this presentation. When we are so critical of
the ideas and images of God which some people have, do
we not run the risk of being left with nothing? After all, is
it not true that all Christians accept the affirmations which
we have made about God? "Is there not room for many
ideas about God," a few people might say, "each one with
his own God?" It appears to me that these questions form
the very core of our theme in these chapters. In our world,
called Western and Christian, and particularly in South
America and in Argentina, "We all believe in God," we are
all Christians. This, however, does not prevent us from seeing life and the world from points of view that are dia-
metrically opposed to each other. The important thing is
to clarify what it means to believe in God, to be a Christian.
The major problem which we confront is not those who do
not believe or who belong to another religion—they are
few, and they are not the worst ones! The major problem is
the indecision and confusion about what we ourselves as
Christians believe. The most urgent task is to clarify for

ourselves what the Christian faith really is, who the God is whom we adore and in whom we profess to believe. Therefore the main problem is not whether we believe or do not believe, but *in which God we believe.*

In the Bible God has an identity that is his own and nontransferable. It is God himself who has defined his identity and his purpose in creation, in the liberation of the people of Israel from slavery, in the law which he gave to his people, in the message of the prophets. It is fundamentally and definitively God who has given us to know Jesus Christ and has built a community to reveal his will and purpose. It is this God, and no other, who is being discussed. One would almost have to say that it is a pity that we have to call him "God," because this is such a general word that seems to include anything to which we assign supernatural properties. It even embraces the character of God himself. The Old Testament speaks of *Yahweh,* the God who revealed himself in a distinct manner, because he is as he is, and he doesn't want to be confused with any other.

I believe that there is a kind of indispensable Christian intransigence in this respect. If people want to put their faith in or adore a god who is seated in the heavens like an impartial and disinterested overseer to what is happening on earth, they certainly can do that. If others want to give the name god to an impersonal spiritual principle or an eternal mind which thinks its own thoughts, in perpetual contemplation of itself, that is their right. If others seek refuge in a god who justifies slavery and human oppression, who approves of and guarantees an unjust order, or who is only concerned with the internal life or the external death, we can't stop them. But we should insist that *these gods are not the God of Jesus Christ,* not the God of the Bible. They are not the God whose message the church has received. This kind of honesty is fundamental so that religion should be merely the mantle which covers any kind of idea, belief, or conduct. The Christian faith has as its axis the God who has defined his identity. Anything else is "to take his name in vain." This is the dividing line of the Christian message.

How to Know?

This is the God proclaimed by the Christian faith. But how does one know if it is the truth or if it is another human invention? We could point out—and we will at some time in our conversations—the authenticity of this God by indicating the most profound and real feeling in our human existence: the desire for love and justice. But, in the final analysis, there is no possible guarantee. The most profound and decisive things in life are never guaranteed to us. We take a risk, like going on an adventure, with the wife or husband whom we marry, or with the child we have and must raise, with the way of life we choose. We can only prove it when we do it. They only become certain when they are put into practice. Whoever doesn't take risks will never know the aspects which make one's life human.

This is what happens in relationship to God. Anyone who isn't prepared to risk himself or herself will never "know." The Bible offers us the way, it invites us into a society with this God. Those who are prepared to start out on this path, to dedicate themselves to this society, confirm this truth. This is the dilemma of the faith. We will never have more faith than when we are ready to practice a total commitment. Faith is not something that people can keep in a pocket and present like a pass when it's necessary. It is a total commitment. With this God there is no "trial marriage." In truth, there never is. A trial marriage only proves the trying, not the marriage. No one could ever convince us that we did not have a marriage if we had truly risked everything, burned all our bridges. The measure is the risk which we are prepared to take. What we have kept to ourselves and not risked will never be tried. And God doesn't accept this kind of behavior. The faith is like the strength of a muscle; we are only aware of it when we use it. The only faith is in the performance of the faith. The noted artist, physician, and pioneer, Albert Schweitzer, concluded his scholarly *The Quest of the Historical Jesus* with:

> He comes to us as One unknown, without a name, as of old, by the lake-side, He came to those men who knew Him not. He speaks to us the same word: "Follow thou me!" and sets us to the tasks which He has to fulfil for our time. He commands. And to those who obey Him, whether they be wise or simple, He will reveal Himself in the toils, the conflicts, the sufferings which they shall pass through in His fellowship, and, as an ineffable mystery, they shall learn in their experience Who He is. (Albert Schweitzer, *The Quest of the Historical Jesus,* trans. W. Montgomery. New York: Macmillan, 1957).

2
DO HUMAN BEINGS EXIST?

Is this not an absurd question? We can doubt the existence of God but is there anything more real than human beings? Nevertheless, it seems to me that we are constantly becoming more doubtful and unsure, in practice as well as in theory, of the existence of people, of the reality of human life *as human life*, as something that has reality and meaning, as something important that we must be aware of. Let us take a few moments to try to understand this.

The Apogee and Objective of Humanity

What we call the modern world, namely, the culture which appeared and developed primarily in Europe and then spread out in all directions at the end of the Middle Ages around the fifteenth and sixteenth centuries, was characterized by an abounding enthusiasm for man, for the human. After centuries in which humanity had been obsessed with the supernatural, the divine and the satanical, caught up in the nostalgia for heaven and the terror of hell, all attention converged on earth and human life. It was time to stop dreaming about the celestial and become firmly planted on earth. The earth had to be transformed into a beautiful place to live for the most noble and creative of inhabitants—the human being. The theme of humanity itself, they insisted, is human beings.

In science, in art, in philosophy, human beings began to conquer themselves and their world. And the results were soon seen. The adventures of the great discoveries widened their horizons. Distances were shortened. New sources of energy provided muscles with almost unlimited power, and scientific exploration uncovered the secrets of creation. At the same time, our thoughts were analyzing the conspiracy of our social and economic relations and were discovering the functions of power, the ways of controlling and organizing it. Politics stopped being powers mysteriously invested in some privileged human beings and was transformed into something potentially open to all reasonably intelligent individuals. The future person was going to be liberated from mere chance, from "natural" contingencies, so that the self could be devoted to exploration. The image of human beings firmly rooted in this world, confident, master of all things was the result of this great movement which deferred interest from the heavens to earth, from God to humanity.

One should not see in these words the nostalgia of a priest for a time and world which lived for God and the heavens. Because if what we said in the preceding chapter about God is true, then this change responds, precisely, to divine will. God didn't say when he created human beings: "Look at the sky and think about me," but rather: "Fill the earth and have dominion over it." God gave us the world and humanity as the fundamental boundaries for our interest and mission. As Christians, therefore, we cannot but participate in the joy and enthusiasm of this modern world which energetically accepts this earthly vocation. No one who has attentively listened to the message of the Bible can dream of a return to that fascination, that obsession with the divine and the satanic, to that renunciation of knowledge, dominion, and transformation of the world. To renounce the earthly vocation is to renounce the divine vocation.

It is, therefore, with no satisfaction, and with profound disappointment and pain that we confirm the progressive deterioration of people in our times. The manifestations of this deterioration acquire dramatic character. What does it mean when a great power like the United States, following a totally coherent and deliberate policy, does not hesitate to destroy a nation and annihilate the animal and vegetable life of vast areas, as was done in Vietnam? And what should one think about the degradation which that act had on those upon whom it was taken—as the witnesses to the Vietnam war have so clearly demonstrated? What value can be assigned to humans in light of these actions?

Or how can one evaluate the industrialization program through which, in the decade of the twenties, the government of the Soviet Union liquidated millions of peasants? Or the massive repressive actions which, in one country or another, did not hesitate to imprison, torture, or assassinate millions of innocent people with the excuse that this was the only way of identifying some presumably guilty individuals?

Yet it is not necessary to speak of such spectacular and dramatic deeds (although they are in no way extraordinary, since they are common practice in many nations). It is enough to ask ourselves what value have persons been given in our system of values, a system which is becoming more and more controlled by technological and economical considerations. You might ask, when a new product is placed on the market if it truly would benefit those who need it most or if it would require materials or elements which could be of better use to a greater number of people? Or are they only thinking of the financial gain they could reap? Are people in our society considered in terms of their creative potential or are they only producers or consumers?

According to bourgeois capitalistic individualism or communistic state bureaucracy, human beings end up being programmed, manipulated machines depersonalized to the point that even in their free moments, their amusement or recreational time is dictated by a structure from which it is difficult to escape—although they are often not even aware of it. Do people really exist for the social, political, or economic organization of our age?

Not even religion escapes this eager manipulation. People end up being considered as some kind of "consumers of religious products" ("peace of the spirit," "salvation," "eternal life" are announced and proclaimed like so many other products in a consumer society). It gives the impression, in many cases, that the churches are more interested in achieving mass consumption of their products than in reaching the deepest depths of need or potential of the people and groups of people for whom they were designed. At times we do not seem to be too concerned that people should find themselves in the faith, hope, and charity of the gospel and become what they should and can become in God; for example, when they consider religion as a "standard" product, a kind of spiritual bath, almost like a toothbrush or a gargle to be used before retiring. Are people really present in many of the stereotyped and impersonal religious activities which we plan, or are they only an organization or product whose success we wish to assure?

It is meaningful to think that the era which began with the exaltation of human beings seems to be closing with their annihilation. The art of the Renaissance, for example, revealed a new discovery, the human form. With what care and passion did Leonardo, among others, discover and treat each detail of that marvelous harmony of form and movement which was the body of man and woman! Today, on the other hand, Picasso's people are fragmented figures, incapable of being harmonized or integrated. The painter becomes here a witness—implacable and unenticing—to the destruction of human beings. The image of men and women vanishes and seems to disappear on the horizon of our humanity.

Image of God

When the Bible relates—in a poetic and figurative way—the creation of the world, it pauses attentively at humans. Here creation reaches its culmination, its center. Here is seen the full intention of the Creator and the dynamics of his plan. Of each act of creation it was said that "it was good." But when God completed his work and placed the human being in the center of creation, entrusted with duty and conferred with dignity, it was said that "everything was very good." God was happy with what he had done. And he was especially happy with human beings. This is the most important and central affirmation that there is for becoming a Christian. Later we will have to talk about evil, disobedience, and corruption. But we should never forget that for God, people are a source of satisfaction and joy.

The first thing that can be said of human beings is that they were made "in the image and likeness of God," in the shape and proportions of the Creator. The significance of these words has been greatly discussed, and each time it becomes clearer that they refer to the three dimensions of human life. The first is the unique relationship of human beings with God. God addresses them directly and awaits their response. With humans he has entered a new covenant—beings who from that point on will be associated with the Creator in the preservation and transformation of the world. God, as we have said, has given space for free

and responsible beings, for *another* who can "listen" and
"respond," who has the gift of "words," a term which has
also been assigned a real and creative power. Adam "will
give names to all the beasts of the earth." And God himself
will respect that word and will call the beasts of the earth
by the names that Adam has given them.

Which brings us to the second element of this image:
humans are "master" of creation, not with the arbitrary and
despotic authority of a tyrant but with the creative and
responsible power of one who can and should elevate that
creation to its fullness and fruition. It is a true power: our
work is not a simple necessity; it is the means by which we
"subject" the world and it "is served" by us; and when we
do this, it gives us meaning and unity. God's world is our
world. And our world is God's world.

This dual relationship of human beings with God and
with the world derives its content and meaning from a third
trait: God did not create and does not desire human beings
who are alienated and alone, but rather a human community with companionship, harmony, and love. For this
reason, the Bible stories tell us, he created "man and
woman." This relationship surpasses a simple biological
function; it is concerned with "one flesh," a total unity.
There is no truly *human* life in an isolated individual,
only in the relationship of mutual exchange, responsibility,
and care of which the human couple is the initial model
and nucleus which extends to all relationships and social
structures. Be they in the economic, political, or communal
sphere, people are not "within themselves" but rather in
relationship to others, which means: we are human beings
in and through love. Human unity does not mean the individual within himself but rather within the community, and
the community is not a mere impersonal aggregate but a
responsible and creative relationship of love. This is no

accident. "God is love" and for that reason he created the world and for that reason he created human beings.

Humanity: A Work in Progress

Human beings and world are related, correlative, inseparable, and complementary terms. God did not make the world like some kind of finished and unalterable machine, or "manufactured toy" for man's diversion, but rather like a garden to be cultivated, able to bear fruit, to produce life, to grow, and to perfect itself. When he said that the world was "good" he did not mean that it was statically finished but rather that "it served his purpose"; it was dynamically rich and inviting, with infinite possibilities; and its development was entrusted to humankind.

Yet this isn't a one-way street. People are also a work in progress. At the same time as they are transforming creation, they are transforming themselves. People also "are well made," not like a statue or a machine but with the potential for growth, for maturity. This is demonstrated by the work which they do in cultivating creation and in communal relationships through which new possibilities for demonstrating this love of the common cause are opened up. While they are cultivating nature, new possibilities for living in a community are opening up to people.

The discovery of fire, for example, provided human beings with progressive new aspects to their lives: conquering the cold, having a circle of light for protection in the night, forging new arms and utensils. And at the same time it provided new possibilities for sociability and culture; re-uniting the family, telling and retelling the stories of their origin and the deeds of the past where they found their roots and identity. Here was a new energy to take care of and manage. It was also a new means of destruction, irresponsibility, and cruelty to the world—burning forests, destroying life—and to his neighbor. Humanity is not made of love alone or fire alone. It is made of love and fire together.

The state of creativity which accompanies the inauguration of modern humankind has, in a very short time, increased all these possibilities. Our ancestors could scarcely care for anyone besides the people who were closest to them—their family, their neighbors, the immediate community. All others were outside their sphere of knowledge and reach. But now the entire world is at our side. When we buy or sell, travel or write, we set in motion a series of circumstances which affect hundreds of millions of people: workers in Japan or Indonesia, European or American financial consortiums, the leaders and peoples of the Arabic nations—and at the same time, in a chain reaction, other hundreds of millions who are dependent on them. This does not occur miraculously, but rather through the understanding of the economic and political mechanism; we should be aware of the probable results of our actions. Thus, the entire world enters the sphere of our responsibility. When the exploited Mexican grape pickers in California began their struggle, the American people found themselves confronted with a new dilemma. Each pound of grapes that they bought or didn't buy was an act of solidarity either with the exploited workers or with the patrons. A massive rejection of that exploitation reduced sales by 40 percent in the United States. The boycott was very effective. But the wine dealers began to innundate the European market with the excess. Thus the European buyer was forced to include in his area of responsibility these unknown Mexican peons who were struggling thousands of miles away.

To be a person is a possibility which is gradually becoming at once richer and more complex: it no longer simply means cultivating our garden, taking care of my husband or wife, educating my children, and being a good neighbor. Now we have to assume responsibility for the world—to know how its resources are used, to know the different organizational and planning possibilities—and participate in the political and educational organizations through which our neighbors, our family, our community and many others will either be made human or will be harmed or destroyed. The human being increases in possibilities, the concept of humanity is enriched each time we discover new areas of realization. This is what God desired for creation: beings who could widen his field of creativity and love until it embraced the entire world and—who knows?—maybe some day, the universe. Why should anyone be afraid of it, if that is a field which God has opened to us to make us complete human beings?

Sin?

Our vision of human life would be distorted and deceitful if we maintained such rosy optimism. Because what effectively happens every time a new possibility for becoming human arises or for placing the fire in the services of love, is that there also arises a possibility for dehumanizing, for increasing the power of destruction and separation. Every area of responsibility is also a potential area of irresponsibility. And the tragedy of humanity is that these means of destruction, of irresponsibility, of dehumanization are equally realized. This is what we call sin.

To sin is to dehumanize, to close off to acts of love—a responsibility which God provides us in the world. It is significant that when Jesus disagreed with the different groups of people around him, the reason was always that one or a group of them irresponsibly and selfishly took possession of relationships or human possibilities which were intended to be shared lovingly. Let us look at three typical cases.

Several times Jesus got involved in the discussion of how sex is related to sin: Is it legal to divorce your wife? What should be done to a woman caught committing adultery? How could Jesus permit a sinful woman to be close to him? In all these cases, Jesus was enormously compassionate toward the woman and very harsh on the man: no sinful woman could be close to him and not be forgiven. However, when someone asked him about the man who, following their custom, could summarily dismiss his wife, he responded very sternly. The man who looks at a woman lasciviously has already committed adultery. Why? Because, to use a concrete example from their society and their time (and isn't it also true in ours?), it was the man who was taking advantage, for his own selfish and irresponsible satisfaction, of a relationship which God had created for the exercise of generous and responsible love. That is sin—sin against God because his plan for the humanization of love is being prostituted.

Jesus engaged in a harsh battle with the religious leaders of the people about their religious customs. God had instituted and ordained a day of rest, of prayer and religious observance, to give people the freedom to turn toward him, to have an ambience of freedom in his presence, to know that God listened to and accepted them despite their weaknesses, to restore their relationship with God. These religious observances should have been a constant witness to divine love, the seal which meant that God did not renounce his society with humanity, the call to be responsible for one's neighbor. But these religious leaders had turned them into an instrument of domination, a means of oppressing the people through fear; they wielded the law like a sword in order to subjugate the conscience of the people, to justify themselves and make themselves appear superior to a nation already overwhelmed with obligations, lacking in resources, and unable to comply with all the laws.

Finally, Jesus showed himself to be harsh on the rich. He was not an ascetic: he liked to eat and drink, to go to parties and partake of a banquet. He didn't want to deprive himself of all that God had created. But, while the rich enjoyed their banquet, poor Lazarus had to content himself with the crumbs that fell from the table. And here is the sin: God set the table of the world for all his children. The selfish appropriation of that table by some is a rejection of God's plan.

Sin is not as much an insult to God himself as it is an insult to God through his children. It is to irresponsibly seize—before future generations—an opportunity which God has given us to become more human, more responsible, and more joyful in his love. Deep down, we understand this very well. When humanity looks for symbols of the truly human, models of what we ought to achieve as human beings, we realize that devoting oneself to others out of love is an essential human quality. The models we find are very different. Among young people, the names Albert Schweitzer, Martin Luther King, and Che Guevara come up, depending on the different ideologies, surroundings, or spheres of influence of the young people. Yet the explanation is always the same: they lived for others and were ready to give their lives for others. Although we may be depressed by the weight of the alienation caused by selfishness, or a destructive and dehumanizing social and economic organization, we still can't help but feel the call of true humanity. We honor those who are trying to build a world out of love and fire, through their work and solidarity.

Freedom to Begin Again

One of my colleagues and a fellow theology professor used to say: "We don't become human beings in order to become Christians; we become Christians in order to be human beings." This statement sums up very well what

Jesus did. His meetings, his cures, his teachings have as their goal the healing of the person—physically, morally, spiritually—so that he or she will be able to live more fully and realize the human vocation. Once when a paralytic was brought to Jesus, he said: "Your sins are forgiven." And when the priests around him became scandalized (because "only God can forgive sins") he changed his statement to: "Rise, take up your bed and go home." Then he asked: "Which of the two things is easier to say?" (Matt. 9:2–5). The lesson is obvious: God and therefore Jesus was sincerely concerned for this man: the forgiveness and physical cure are two dimensions of the same healing. Through both of them, it is God himself who is present and acting. The two things together put the man back on his feet and restored him to life (to his home). The encounters of Jesus with the people are never the end of the road but rather the point of departure. It may seem that he invited them to follow him, that he ordered them to sell all they had, that he sent them out healed of their infirmities to return to their land and their families. But what he really did was take imprisoned people and put them back on course, in the direction of a fuller humanity in regard to their health, integration with the community, vocation—in the final analysis, in the direction of the kingdom of God, which is the fullness of humanity and the world.

Human beings exist. They exist as the plan of God. They exist for work and for love, for responsible human community which gratefully and fully exists on the earth which has been given to them as their property and for the common good of the human family. People are on their way— torn between their vocation and its negation, anxious to become completely human, but losing their way a thousand times in their eagerness for irresponsible and selfish dominion over the world and other persons, trying to realize their humanity through shortcuts, robbing and seizing what has already been freely given to them. Men and women exist in hope because God puts them on their way again and again, and God restores their freedom to work and to love. The Christian message is a call to accept that freedom; not to be supermen or demigods, but rather to live like human beings in the presence of God, to be lovingly responsible for the world and for other human beings.

THEMES FOR REFLECTION

The Church and Humanization

"Is the church truly humanized? Isn't it true that the church has often tried to shape people, to make them resign themselves to their condition?" Conversely, one might ask, "Isn't it really politics which permits people to assume their responsibility?"

These two questions come from different points of view and appear to be quite dissimilar. Nevertheless, I believe that they are complementary. As critics of the church—self-criticism by those who are part of it—we ought to keep an adequate historical perspective, derived from the affirmation that our human vocation is "to humanize"—to place in the service of the community in single-minded love any new possibility which arises from the responsible use of the world. From modern times on, as we have said, these possibilities have been given in increasing rhythm. But we must remember that in ancient times, most people endured their history instead of making it. Not only because some were evil and oppressed the masses, but more certainly because the abundance of resources which we have today was not yet possible. Most people had no other recourse (not only because of injustice but also because of real limitations) than to spend most of their lives eking out a minimal existence from the soil, scarcely above the level of starvation and disease. The other areas of life—culture,

knowledge, recreation—for the majority of the people, I repeat, due to objective conditions and not only oppression
were limited to a few occasions. It is not that there were
only rich and poor—which is true—but that all humanity
was hopelessly poor.

Under such conditions, political participation, which
means the possibility of active participation by the whole
community in their own destiny, remained, with few ex-
ceptions, outside the realm of possibility. There was no way
for the entire community to organize itself and carry out
their plan. They had, rather, to endure their history. More
than once, the church helped the masses to endure history
with a certain joy and hope. It helped them to believe that
the horizons of their lives were not closed in by the poverty
and misery of the present but would be opened up to an
eternity. It gave them a human dimension, although it was
projected into another life which could only be manifested
here as resignation. If we mean to say by this that it was
the "opium of the people," then we can. But a responsible
physician doesn't discontinue the use of a drug when the
subsequent pain is useless and even destructive.

We are not trying to pass judgment on the past. Ours is
a different problem. Because, while new possibilities were
being opened up, when the sicknesses caused by misery,
destitution, or impotence became curable for vast sections
of the world, the church continued to sleep. It forgot
its human vocation and lent itself to the service of those
who were irresponsibly amassing for themselves those
things that belonged to the whole human family. Today
there is no objective reason why the whole world cannot
feed itself, protect itself from sickness and abandonment,
achieve a level of freedom and recreation, actively participate in their own roles and in their families' lives. Those
who would have us believe that we are condemned to in-
equality and misery lie in order to defend their selfish class
or racial egotism behind a facade of technical and rational

appearances which, in fact, are schemes leading to disaster. When this occurs, Christians, since they are responsible for announcing and participating in the Creator's plan, are irrevocably obligated to denounce this situation and to make an effort to change it. The transformation of human conditions in a complex society like ours, is a *political* task. Thus, obedience to the Creator's mandate is unavoidably passed on today through political action.

Yet the church has continued to live in the pre-modern world where people were resigned to endure history. And what is even worse, it christens this suffering with the name "will of God." When it does this, it puts the divine seal of approval on an inhuman condition and becomes God's enemy. These terms may appear too strong; however, it is difficult not to arrive at this conclusion. Any possibility for the enrichment of human life is a gift from God. To take it away or to prevent anyone from enjoying it is to go against divine will. The church has failed people with its deceit: it has not given men and women their true image, it has not projected the image from the Bible on reality, and therefore it has kept up the image of human beings as resigned to their fortune. To the optionless person whose hope is minimized by external forces, the church has been an "opium" when it should have been a "tonic." And as a result of this, it has produced in its own midst, men and women who are incapable of assuming their human responsibility, people with a mentality of "resignation," filled with the kind of attitude which some have called "social repose."

Humanity and Politics

There are those who protest each time a preacher or a theologian "meddles in politics." It is quite possible that we have sinned more than once by attempting to make judgments and define positions without the necessary technical competence, and as a result we have made no sense. But if politics is the action through which the human community assumes and completes its duty of planning their lives, determining their goals, and organizing themselves to achieve this, how could Christians renounce this concept? How could they remain silent on this topic, especially when they see that the world is being taken away from them? Politics is the attempt at retrieving the world for people, at seizing power from the irrational, from the high-handedness of an inhuman system, and of then restoring it to its original proposition—to serve the enrichment and fullness of the human community. And this is a fundamental Christian obligation. You can't be a Christian without accepting it, because you can't be a human being without doing it.

This does not mean, however, that the whole world should have political activity as its specific vocation. This is a very important dilemma in vocational ethics which we should put aside for the moment. The point in question here is whether or not the image of the human being is in our times the image of a political person, or rather, those who assume responsibility for the rest of the community, who try to understand and dedicate themselves to processes through which the community is structured and modified and who fulfill this responsibility and this understanding throughout their entire lives, whether in their vocational fields or their families, in their cultural or religious life. In this sense, a true human being *politics* all his or her life.

Has the church fulfilled its duty as "comforter"? I don't think so. Mere awareness of one's responsibility and duty without joyful and confident acceptance of the limitations and failures of those who accept the human undertaking, can only produce frustration and desperation. The Christian faith means these limitations can be accepted without paralyzing individuals because they are taking on a project over which God is watching, risking their own lives to realize it and which can turn their lives completely around without the fear of failure. We will return to this topic in the next chapter.

Humanity and the Cosmos

"Does Christian thought—theology—contemplate a *cosmic* projection of man?" The Bible naturally speaks of the "earth" as the home of human beings. And theology has traditionally made it so. Some have concluded from this that humans are forbidden to leave earth and go into outer space. It would be an invasion of "heaven," God's space, and therefore an irreligious undertaking which is doomed to fail.

This point of view is attributed more to the pagan religions, against which the biblical message rather than the thinking of the Scripture is directed. Of course, the biblical authors, who lived some two or three thousand years ago, never dreamed of space exploration. However, neither did they deify the firmament, and this is very important. While neighboring peoples considered the sun, the moon, and the stars as divine beings to be honored, and upon which their destiny depended (how many people even today consult their horoscopes!), the Bible considered them as part of creation, just like the earth. "God created the heavens and the earth," the Bible says and the Creed reiterates. The heavens and the earth signify "everything, the totality of what exists," the universe, the cosmos. They constitute creation itself. And it is therefore a space open to people. When they discover it, or simply delight in contemplating it, they aren't invading forbidden territory, they aren't infringing on God's privileges. They are performing their human vocation. The only question is whether they are doing it responsibly, whether they are truly using the fire— the spaceships, the probings, the knowledge—in the service of love. It is no better or worse to misuse the moon than to misuse the ocean or the public marketplace. Even if some day other created beings appear on our horizons, our responsibility would be the same—the transformation of the world in the service of love. It is not necessary to speculate about that possibility today. With that new discovery, new possibilities "to be human" would open up, perhaps new possibilities for community, for solidarity, for creativity. A true Christian should try to respond to this new gift with gratitude. The extent of the cosmos is not determined by an arbitrary boundary fixed by God but rather by the dynamics of human action which God has made possible and which he continues to make possible and encourage.

Perfection and Maturity

"What is this human fullness which we have been talking about?" We could define it in the same terms we used in talking about the "image of God," which we mentioned earlier. But we can also remember some of Jesus' thoughts: "Be perfect as your Father who is in heaven is perfect" (Matt. 5:48). The word "perfect" can also mean "mature" or "complete." The same statement of Jesus appears in another gospel like this: "Be merciful, even as your Father is merciful" (Luke 6:36). Whatever the original statement, or perhaps both statements, the meaning is the same. Jesus had been saying that the love of God is practiced without discrimination against anyone; divine providence is universal. And it concludes: "May you also be." Christian perfection is not an abstract or static perfection; it is the struggle to elevate the totality of humanity and the world to a responsible and active love. Perfect is the one who loves as God loves. And, as we have seen, the personal life as well as the communal human life is constantly increasing in the sphere of knowledge and the possibilities of realization. Perfection is the process of *maturity* through which we learn to responsibly express our love and work on each new horizon, in each new relationship, at each new stage of our personal life and of history. "Increase in love until you are full." This is the meaning of the human.

It is worthwhile to add—although it is obvious—that when we speak of love we are not referring to a mere feeling or emotion, but to a concrete and effective commitment to the real need of another or others who have been placed in our sphere of action. Love is a disposition or an effective desire which is lived out intelligently and concretely every day. The search for perfection is, then, the struggle to include totality within the effective action of my love through the possibilities that are opened up to me.

3

IS THERE LIFE
BEFORE DEATH?

This isn't an editorial error or a misprint. This question actually appeared on a wall in one of the most devastated sections of the city of Belfast in Northern Ireland. "Is there life before death?" Amidst the violence that has been erupting there for the past few years, where at any moment a bomb can explode in a supermarket or on a crowded street in the middle of the afternoon, where anyone can suddenly be shot down by a machine gun or sniper's bullet, where only one thing is certain—the risk of death—a terrorized nation asks itself: Is life possible under such conditions? Is there a life that can be lived *before* death?

In contrast to other periods, people today believe that this life, before death, is what is important. The longing and the hope for an afterlife were characteristic of previous people, but we are interested in this life. In response to a question in a televised interview, one gentleman commented: "They have given me a pass to this function and if it is postponed because of rain I can't return it; I have to take advantage of this ticket because it is the only one I have."

Now Is the Time

In biblical terms, our gentleman wasn't far from the truth. His statement was more profound than he himself realized. This is the life we have been given. Here and now our life is being played out. It is astonishing how little the

Bible speaks of the other life. We twist it around because
we feel convinced that it should be that way. But the ex-
pressions that we interpret as referring to a life after death,
such as "eternal life" or "life in Christ" or even "heavenly
life" were actually a reference to this life. "This is the
eternal life," said Jesus, "that you may know the one true
God and Jesus Christ whom he sent" (John 17:3). And
this occurs, as the gospel clearly indicates, here and now.
Let us also examine the famous passage in Colossians in
which the reader is exhorted to: "Turn your attention to
heavenly things, not the things of the earth" (3:2). Here
we surely have a passage that refers to the "other life."
And as if to confirm it, he adds: "because your life is hid
with Christ in God." But to our astonishment, he continues:
"Put to death therefore what is earthly in you," and he
begins to distinguish *earthly* from *heavenly* things. Lust,
greed, lies, and hatred are all earthly things, while compassion, meekness, discipline, and forgiveness are heavenly
things. Social, religious, or racial discrimination are elements of the former, and peace and solidarity belong to the
latter. And so that no one continues to be deceived the
author begins to list the circumstances and relationships
under which one should live this new life, the heavenly life
in family, marital, and work relationships. It is evident that
the "heavenly" life has a very "earthly" boundary.

In Jesus' time, there was a sharp controversy among the
Jews over the resurrection of the dead. One group, the
Sadduccees, denied it while the other group, the Pharisees,
believed in it. They discussed the nature of life after the
resurrection and whether those who died went after a time
to the "bosom of Abraham" or directly to "paradise." Jesus
affirmed several times the reality of the resurrection. But it
is interesting that Jesus gave particular emphasis to the
parable (probably a well-known story) that he used to
clarify this question. He told them about the rich man who

gave a banquet every day and during the banquet a beggar
named Lazarus would pick up the crumbs from the banquet table. Both men died; the rich man went to the place
of torment and the poor man went to the bosom of Abraham. The rich man begged for Lazarus to come and allevi-
ate his suffering, or at least for permission to return and
warn his family of what lay ahead for them. The response
to his pleas was harsh and sharp: the decisive moment has
already passed. Eternity was already at work while he had
been enjoying his life without caring about his fellow man.
The character and destiny of his life was sealed then and
there. The wall which had been built between them could
not be torn down now. The message is clear. This was not
a discussion of the resurrection or the future life. It is a
story that reveals the contrast between the rich and the poor
which we ourselves perpetuate. Think about what happens
in this life and this world. One is the result of the other.

The real question is whether or not here, in this life, we
participate in the "society" which God has established with
human beings for the creation and transformation of the
world. Here and now we either accept or reject the invitation and challenge. Here and now we either participate
or not in God's plan. This life here is the decisive factor.

God has given me a pass for this life and he will not take
it back if I do not do well. Or, to use the simile which
Jesus used, they have given me a "talent" to cultivate and
help bear fruit. If I bury it out of fear or negligence, I have
buried myself with it. This life is the theme of the Bible.

But Is There Really One Life?

This is our dilemma: the emptiness or the fullness of this
life. Can we speak of the years which we spend on this
earth as "one life" or are they only a series of more or less
casual disconnected experiences without meaning? Do we
live one life or are we only "getting by" from one day to

the next until death surprises us? Does our life have meaning?

Allow me to get personal for a minute. When someone turns fifty and begins to view his life as something already defined and determined, like a well traveled road, he begins to ask a question with some urgency. Can I really consider my life as a unity with meaning and direction? If I look at it objectively and dispassionately, must I answer: "I am not sure that it is like that." There are so many disconnections, so many gaps, so many dead-end streets! How many times did I have to tear out the page and start again? My intention of a few months ago to write an article developing this thought renewed this impression: after I revised some things I had written at least two decades ago, how many inconsistencies, how many indecisions, how many starts and stops there were!

Is my life really *one* life? Are there battles which I fight with all my strength, which take years, and about which I can only ask sincerely: "Were they really that important? Were they really worth it?" If I try to evaluate them objectively, I must admit that I can't answer these questions with any certainty. I suppose that the same thing, more or less, happens to all of us. It isn't that there are not significant events in our lives. There are, and when we look back we cannot help but realize it. We have learned something over the years. There are things which we see clearly, convincingly. We have worked and we have succeeded in some areas of our work. There are things which we have done well, and which have remained well-done. Some of the causes we fought for were worth it, and are still important. And we are prepared to continue fighting for them. Above all, we have loved and been loved. And this is probably the most important thing. We have had parents, a spouse, brothers and sisters, children, friends, companions whom we still have and hold dear. But all of this does not erase the question: Are all these things *one* life? Do they have continuity? Do they have coherence? Do they have a future? Or are they only a spark in the night without any future or meaning?

Love Will Never Cease to Be

I think that this is the true problem of hope. The apostle Paul has an answer to the question. In one of his most famous passages, he speaks of the faith through which, even in darkness, we trust in the power of God. He speaks of the hope through which we "stretch" ourselves toward that quality of life which Christ showed us and offered us. But when we have to speak of the permanent quality of that faith and that hope, of what really gives meaning and continuity to everything, we must concentrate on only one thing—love. Faith and hope will pass away, but love endures. The most heroic actions, the most philanthropic or resounding deeds, can be nothing more than short-lived manifestations of an action with no value or permanence. They can be the isolated sound of an instrument played thoughtlessly. Only love gives permanence and meaning to these actions. Because only in love is there the permanence, the tenacity, the total commitment, the prudence, and the sensitivity which can achieve a permanent result. There is one life if there is love and in the extent to which there is love. We repeat the words of the Uruguayan theologian, J. L. Segundo, which we cited before, that the gospel can be summed up in a single statement: "There is no love lost in this world."

Jesus makes the same affirmation in two notable passages. The first tells of the woman (tradition has identified her as Magdalene) who approached Jesus and anointed him with expensive oil. The disciples mumbled about this "waste," and Jesus defended her by telling them that she had performed an act of love (to anoint someone who is going to die is one of the acts of mercy). Then he added this beautiful and serious statement: "Truly I tell you that wherever

in the world the message of salvation is preached, they will
also tell of this woman, so that she will be remembered"
(Mark 14:9). To a small act of love is assigned the same
importance as to the gospel's message of salvation. It has
been said that that small act has the same nature as salvation itself, as permanent, as eternal as the gospel itself.
Whenever they speak of the love of God, this woman and
her act of love will be present. With that act of love, she
became immortal. Because love, like God's word itself, is
eternal, and with his word an act of love will never be without a future.

The other passage is the parable of the judgment from
Matthew 25, in which the Son of man separates the "sheep"
from the "goats," the accepted from the rejected. The cri-
terion for the judgment was proclaimed in two statements:
"You did . . . ," "You did not. . . ." What? Once again, acts
of love (which every Jew had learned to recognize since
infancy): to give food to the hungry, to give drink to the
thirsty, to clothe the naked, to visit and care for the imprisoned, the stranger, the sick. And once again, it is
judged in relationship to Jesus Christ himself: "Inasmuch
as you did it (or did not do it), to the least of my brethren,
you did it (or did not do it), to me." There is no act of
love that is lost, without an eternal future. We deceive ourselves if we see this as a simple commercial transaction; for
a service offered to a poor person here, you receive a reward later there. It is concerned with the very nature of the
future which Jesus Christ offers. His kingdom is the triumph
of single-minded and active love. Every act which corresponds to this kingdom has eternal permanence, is made
of the same material as the kingdom itself, and therefore is
included in it. In the New Testament there is little speculation about death and the hereafter. What is constantly repeated is that the love of Jesus Christ is permanent and
that death cannot end it. Therefore, Jesus Christ gives an
eternal dimension to the love in our lives. Whoever has

identified himself with it has already conquered death.

One more episode from the gospel should be mentioned in this regard. As Jesus was approaching a city one day, he met the funeral cortege of a young man, an only child, and his mother came to Jesus' side crying. Jesus felt sorry for her and restored her son to life and "gave him to his mother" (Luke 7:15). The focus of this passage is not simply the power of Jesus to restore life, but also it is Jesus' compassion in restoring a future to the broken love of the mother. The son would die at another time; the mother would also. What is shown and proven here is that, in Christ, love does not have to cry over what seems lost. Whoever lives in love here in this life has a future both here and in eternity.

There is no other answer to the question of life after death. It belongs to the same reality as this life. We have *one* life on this side of death—not a meaningless series of isolated moments or episodes—because of and in the extent to which we participate in the reality of love. And since this love is not a mere human manifestation, but an overflow of feeling that has as its impetus and foundation *the very being of God,* life has an eternal future. The meaning of our life before death and our belief in a life after death has one single guarantee: the love of Jesus Christ. We can't look for any other. The love of God and our active acceptance of it constitute the only possibility for one life to arise out of this series of disconnected, often contradictory, thoughts and actions, triumphs and failures; and such a meaningful life must have a future in the afterworld. In love and only in love does our life have a future.

Love Cannot Be Spoken of
in the Singular

It is easy to misunderstand what we have just said, if you imagine humankind as a group of autonomous, independent individuals walking along side by side loving each other and transcending this life to the afterlife. However, such an idea is absurd because love means precisely the breaking down of that individual, autonomous, and independent existence. Therefore to say that the meaning and the reality of life is love is to place it in the human community, in the society of persons—in the only place in which love can assume a body and an expression. However, we don't have to resort to logical deductions to prove this, the Bible is very explicit in this respect. It does not speak of love in the context of isolated individuals or even strictly individual relationships but rather in a context of hope and in the affirmation of the kingdom of God. This is the very core of the Bible and of the message of Jesus.

It isn't necessary to stop here to detail the concept of the kingdom of God; there is abundant material available on this subject. It is enough for us to say that it refers to a humanity that has been transformed on a renewed earth. It is a vision of a world in which the creative plan of God is finally fulfilled; where hunger, poverty, injustice, oppression, pain, even disease and death have been definitively overcome; it is a world from which evil has been rooted out forever. Where the love of God is "all and in all," where the human love manifested in Jesus Christ has penetrated all humankind and therefore fulfills God's plan for creating a humanity which manifests his love in a harmonious world which they themselves work, cultivate, and make fruitful. "Peace and justice" are the two biblical terms which characterize this vision. Justice is the restoration of the proper relationship between people and their dominion over the earth, their concern for the rights of the defenseless and their protection of life. Peace is the condition of both personal and communal fulfillment. Peace is the condition of the family in which each member lives comfortably and happily, working and relaxing in that great home which is the world. This is the biblical vision. This is the spirit which God stresses in the Epistle to the Ephesians where he says that he proposes "to unite all things in him (Jesus Christ)" (Eph. 1:10), which really means, to unify the entire universe with the key of love ("the mystery revealed"). This universal vision of the recreation of the world and of humanity is the recurring theme throughout the entire Bible, in the message of Jesus and in all of Christian hope.

A host of questions arises from this statement: How? When? In what way? How can human achievements be related to divine action through this hope? The Bible responds to these questions with images, parables, symbols, and poetry. There is no "geography" or "chronology" of the kingdom of God in the Bible; nor is there any geography or chronology of the life after death. The Bible uses poetic and symbolic language to help us to perceive the qualities of the future life. It is concerned with a future of *humanity,* of *nations,* or rather of persons in relation to other persons, of a collective and organized existence, of a human society. This is the very essence of the Christian message; to reduce it to a personal or private life and the eternal continuation of that life is to greatly distort this message. A private life, lived in itself and for itself, and prolonged eternally, is, in truth, hell, condemnation, damnation, because love cannot conform to living a private life. The biblical message is one of a community which is created and recreated in love, in a world destined to be "the home" of that community.

We are not encouraged nor are we authorized to speculate about how and when this proposal will be consummated. Jesus told his disciples that such speculation was not their concern. But if this is truly the nature of Christian hope, there is one vitally important consequence: every act, action, or plan which, here and now on this earth, realizes God's plan, even if only partially, will have an eternal future. What we have said about personal acts of love—the anointing with oil or giving food to the hungry, and the like—we must also say about corporate, structural, or organized forms of love. It would be absurd to think that the piece of bread placed in the hand of a beggar is an act of love while the legislation or social organization which would eliminate all hunger is not. Or that a visit to the sick should be considered a service for Jesus while a national health program which would prevent millions of infirmities should not.

If this is so, then we, especially considering our present situation in Latin America today, would have to consider as *part of the gospel* some things that might sound very strange. We would have to admit that all opposition to oppression and injustice must have a future. And for that reason, it is part of our human service to Jesus Christ's opposition to capitalistic greed and bureaucratic dehuman- ization and the substitution of monopolies and multina- tionals for an economy which serves all humankind. It is the struggle to politically organize the human community with a real, not false quality, so that people will have equal value, not just in theory but in actual opportunities for them to develop their abilities and manage their jobs and their lives. It is also a struggle in the name of Christ to liberate women from being treated as "things" so that they can become integral parts of the human unity ("Man and woman he created them") and work in the service of Jesus Christ. Another aspect of this service is the transformation of the educational system into a joy that serves as the humanization of the child. All of these things are part of the fight against sin and the establishment of the kingdom of God.

In this respect, we should also ask ourselves if the thousands of human battles waged to secure small amounts of freedom, justice, or dignity which are often bathed in human blood, often only partially triumphant, and where often the victory itself is deceiving, really constitute history

or merely reflect isolated incidents with no permanent significance. And the answer is always the same. Christians
should not be cynical in regard to human history for the
same reason that they should not be cynical in regard to
their personal life. They have learned to see the power of
love manifested in Jesus Christ to ransom, to perfect, and
to give eternal future to every instant of their personal life
and to every movement in the communal life of human
beings. They have come to see the love of God preserve and
give meaning to all life. God indicates how and when this
fruition is to be fully realized. But God has invited us to
begin to create the future and has promised to guarantee
and certify for eternity what we create through personal
and collective love. There is *one* human history in this
world before death because God is love. And therefore
there is also *one human history* after death and after this
world. This is the nature and foundation of Christian hope.

THEMES FOR REFLECTION

Images of the Future Life

We have indicated the poetic and symbolic character
presented to us in the Bible of the life after death. One of
these images is that of a "repose" or "dream." Because of
this, we have frequently imagined the future life as one of
pure passiveness. Yet the final repose does not really signify
passiveness at all, but rather harmony, tranquillity, seren-
ity, familiarity. When God said to his people: "In repose
you will find your strength," he was not inviting them to
passiveness but rather to a serene familiarity. There is one
image that appears several times in the Bible which has
often been ridiculed: that of the resurrected faithful play-
ing harps and singing in the presence of God in heaven.
This certainly is a childish picture. However, its significance
is very profound; because music and song are the human
activities through which we can most profoundly experi-

ment with the unity of work and pleasure, duty and creation, discipline and freedom, personal experience and communal unity. When we make music, even within our own
limitations, it seems as if the gap that exists between the
effort and the enjoyment disappears. It is as if my own in-
dividuality, without being lost, is united with a common
harmony; I am active and passive at the same time; I myself am at once the chorus and the orchestra. There are
fleeting moments in life when the weight of our labor is
lifted and is transformed into the full expression of our
being. Art and particularly music are magnificent symbols
of this. The future life is present, in this image, like the
kind of life in which effort, work, and service become joy
and repose, while happiness is creation, service, and duty.
Obviously, this is characteristic of a life filled with love.
There is here still another dimension: all of this occurs "in
the presence of God," offered to him as worship, as appre-
ciation. It is interesting that both in Hebrew and in Greek,
the Bible uses the word *service* (work, a fulfilling duty) to
refer to the *worship* of God. To realize my duty joyfully is
to honor God through his plan for me. Once again, the
similarity which we mentioned, unites these three aspects:
my being myself without any obstacles to my enjoyment of
creation, my dedicating myself to the common duty of
creating a unity with others, and my honoring God by
offering him my service and common creation; this is the
true life.

If this is the true life, then any approximation of that
life within the limitations of our world and our history
would be the true Christian mission. This means trying to
transform work by removing those elements that make it a
compulsive burden, thereby allowing ourselves to experience the joy of its realization and its results and the feeling
that it is not some private thing that I have to do, but
rather a realization for the common good. There is here
the basis for an ethics of work and of recreation for the

economical and political fields as well as for the organization of one's personal and communal life. Our vision of the future also encompasses the present. Within these images of the future, there lies hidden a call for the transformation of the present. More than once, these images have been put in the service of a static and negative view of life and the present world. It is the Christian's duty to rescue this vision and give it the dynamic interpretation that it demands.

There is another image which is worth mentioning: that of "reward." Can we speak of the future life as a "reward" for the good performed in this life? Catholics and Protestants have furiously debated this question. We realize that this term is used in the New Testament, but we also realize that the future life—like everything else offered to us in the gospel—is free and nonnegotiable. The error stems from a literal interpretation of the idea of reward as a kind of "credit" which we accumulate in heaven for our actions on earth, a credit which we can collect at a given time. Such an idea is obviously absurd given the situation presented in the Bible. However, if we interpret the word as an image, a kind of parable which teaches that actions that belong to this new life are never incomplete or unfinished, but rather are projected into the future, then the idea seems coherent and positive. What we began to realize in love, although it may be incomplete, is assured its fulfillment by God. Its deficiencies have to be "compensated for," its imperfections purified. Far from being artificial or casual, this is the only response worthy of the God of love; it understands, completes, perfects, gives a future to that which was begun and follows in the same direction as his plan.

Heaven and Hell

One participant in our discussion asked: "It has been said that there is no love lost in this world; if this is true, then is selfishness lost, or hatred? Will selfishness and hatred exist in the future?" I don't believe we should say that hatred and selfishness have a future since having a future means having permanence, meaning, or ultimate reality. It is characteristic of hatred and selfishness to deny the future. They lead to death, destruction, annihilation. In this sense, they and the future are mutually exclusive. Love and hatred can never be symmetrical; one opens up life and therefore has a future, while the other has death as its ultimate end.

When we speak of the "end" of hatred and selfishness, we refer to a very significant idea in the New Testament. The obstinate and tenacious rejection of love has as its end, or consequence, the destruction and death of the individual who has so rejected it. Those who identify themselves with the denial of life at the same time identify themselves with death, and therefore they have no future. This affirmation is very grave. Those who make selfishness and hatred dominant traits in their lives have already denied life and are "dead." The future will only confirm and verify this denial. This is what eternal damnation and judgment mean. They have inherited the death which they chose. This is what hell means.

Love and Conflict

A whole series of questions comes up concerning the concrete conditions in which we are called to exercise love in this world and life. On the one hand, we have to recognize that often the choices we must make are ambiguous: by helping one, we may hurt another; a good deed which we perform may have bad consequences which we can't avoid, even if we try. Some philosophers refer to "compromises" or "concessions" which have to be made on some moral issues. By this they mean that it is impossible to achieve a pure "good." We have to accept "diminutions," hybrids, a lesser good in order to avoid a greater evil. But this is really an artificial problem since the only *real* good is that which we ourselves can *realize,* which we can make concrete and effective. Everything else belongs to a philosophy called "idealism," one which has done a great deal of harm. It maintains that perfect things exist out there, floating in space, and that we must imitate them in our behavior. However, the only sure things that exist in our sphere of activity are concrete conditions, people, and circumstances. The important thing is to respond to them in the most human way possible, to manifest real love in the real world. The real good is the good which we can perform. The important thing is not the imagined distance between what I actually can do and what I *could* do if the circumstances or conditions were different, but rather what I concretely can do *here and now.* My witness as a Christian will be judged on what I do now. The future, the perfection, the "reward" of these decisions and actions are in God's hands.

Some of the young people present asked a question about the relationship between love and conflict. Does love mean that the Christian must avoid all conflict and seek compromises or concessions in every situation? This has often been suggested as the meaning of love. However, a simple look at the Bible or the life of Jesus will demonstrate that this is, at best, a misinterpretation, and, at worst, an outright evil-minded distortion of the biblical message. The life of Jesus is a life of love, and *therefore* of conflict. Or better yet, his love is involved in the conflicting conditions of human life in which it cannot help but take part. This love is involved in the often radical tensions we find in our current international situations, with rich countries and poor countries, oppressors and oppressed, and in the conflicts present within our own societies. It is impossible for one to remain on top of or outside of these tensions. The question is how a love which seeks the total communion of humanity can be related to these conflicts. This topic could lead us to an intricate web of questions which would not be appropriate to discuss at this time. However, it is worth mentioning two or three points for reflection on this theme: 1) The Christian objective is not "conciliation" but "reconciliation," which means that resolution of tension by which justice has been reestablished, and through which the enemies find themselves in the real state of brothers and sisters, not in the position of accepting conditions which would only perpetuate their animosity. In this sense, the "reconciliation" of the oppressors with the oppressed, of the possessors with the dispossessed, requires the transformation of the conditions of oppression. 2) Love seeks that solution of tensions which best respects the humanity of the protagonists, a solution that does the least damage to the individual and to human life, one that plants the conditions for a future of true community. 3) Love tries to respect the human dignity of the enemy even in the midst of the conflict. (At this point we ought to think about the radical nature of God's judgment, one which is always governed by love.) 4) Love understands that in every conflict there should be a transformation of *everyone* who takes part in it. The justice to which we commit ourselves can never mean self-justification or self-idealization. The resolution of the conflict and therefore the conditions which are set down and the way of fighting for them must be a process of transforming our own lives because the cause for which we are fighting (if it is truly the cause of God's love) is always a call for repentance, conversion, and the renewal of what we have attained. 5) The conflicts in which we are involved are not simply struggles between good and evil. They are, in spite of their intensity, *moments* in our progress by which God guides us to the final realization of his plan. This does not mean that they are not important. But it does mean that we cannot concentrate on "one great battle," the totality of the struggle. We make a great mistake if we think that we can ignore the small manifestations of love—personal compassion, consideration, even gentleness and courtesy—while fighting the great battle, the transformation of the whole system. There is, of course, an order of importance. But *reality is only one part*. The great battle is one part of a long campaign. The dramatic decision of the great battle and the daily duty of love are complementary and inseparable dimensions of that life which truly has a future.

A final note on this topic concerns the essential relationship between true love and rationality and organization. True love cannot remain as intention, in the abstract; it demands to be made concrete. However, in order to do this one must choose *a way* to concretize it. We can do this in personal situations by responding to the need of a friend or neighbor or member of the family. However, we have already seen that it does not stop there.

When love is confronted with human need in its widest sense, it must choose a strategy, a political and economic orientation, and become involved in the forms of organization. If love stops short of manifesting itself in this way, it can only with great difficulty be called love. It is for this reason that the Old Testament insists on the law, which is basically an ordination that gives form to a concern for man and for the world. However, for us today this does not mean following those laws of the Bible which correspond to historical circumstances already long since passed but rather understanding the intent of those laws and finding current ways of realizing them. Rationality, which is the search for understanding and organization, is an essential condition in the exercise of love.

4

IS THERE ANY SECURITY?

Throughout this book we have repeated phrases like "for Christians," "in the biblical perspective," "from the point of view of faith," to show that things are this way or that way. In this context, we have spoken of a God who made human beings and society so that they could perfect the world together; and he invested them with a love that knows no limits or failures but is always involved in following his plan for a personal and collective human life. This life has both a present and an eternal future, and is dedicated to the creation of God's love. It is not surprising that someone asked, "Who says so?" Or more precisely, "Who tells me that this is the truth? What assurance do I have that this isn't a romantic dream, very pretty perhaps, but not real?"

This is neither a capricious nor superfluous question. Since, as we have already explained, it is true that at certain moments we perceive in the depths of our being that this is how things ought to be, we also perceive in our daily experience that things are not this way. If unselfish love awakens in our hearts an echo, it also creates an inertia that can cause us to reject it. The experience of rejected love, abandoned solidarity, unreturned generosity, betrayed confidence is one of the most common and shocking experiences in our lives. Do we not witness the daily triumph of underhandedness, the advancement of people who unscrupulously step on others in order to get their way, the large and small tragedies in the lives of individuals and communities? Is not the dance of death at times more prevalent in our world than the victorious song of love? Is there anything in the world that really sustains love, or is it destined eventually to be extinguished? Is love a great illusion? These are not purely rhetorical questions. They are real and profound because the gospel invites us to stake our lives on that God who is the God of human beings, by whom life was created for love and for whom love has a future. If this is not true then we are wasting our lives.

A Gamble . . .

"The gospel invites us to put our lives on the line," as we have said before. The great Christian thinker, Pascal, called it "a gamble." Whether or not we like the metaphor, the meaning is clear. An English author once told an interesting parable to illustrate this very truth. During the last World War, an English citizen wanted to join the French Resistance. In England, he made contact with some agents of the Resistance. Finally he was given a place and a date to meet the chief of the Resistance in French territory. He went to the assigned place and identified himself. The chief of the Resistance asked him numerous questions, and finally accepted him with these strange and disturbing words: "You a foreigner and cannot understand much of what is going on here. You will see strange things. But you should be certain of one thing. I am the chief. And I know what we are doing. Trust me." Time passed. The new recruit saw members of his group in Nazi uniforms, performing missions which seemed to be the exact opposite of their plans. He saw the chief collaborating with the enemy. Could this truly be the Resistance he had joined? Could he be the victim of some monstrous plot? Was the chief a traitor?

In the midst of his doubts, he could only hold on to one thought: "Have confidence in me, and in the end you will see."

This is all that is required by our faith. Jesus of Nazareth tells us to have confidence in him and in the end we will see.

. . . Based on a Life

Jesus took seriously the history of the God of Israel, the God who had proclaimed justice and peace, who had promised a future for humanity and for the world. So seriously did Jesus take him that he lived out that promise all his life, and finally gave up his life for it. One of the prophets of that God foresaw the liberation from oppression, sickness, and poverty. And Jesus used his same words when he announced that "the Spirit of the Lord is upon me, because he has anointed me to preach good news to the poor. He has sent me to proclaim release to the captives and recovery of sight to the blind, to set at liberty those who are oppressed, to proclaim the acceptable year of the Lord" (Luke 4:18–19). A few accepted his message and joined him. And down through the centuries others have done likewise. But there is no contract, no guarantee. Jesus simply says: *"Follow me."*

It is clear, however, that we don't blindly enter into "Jesus' game." His very life is a guarantee because it is impossible to read the story of his life and not feel the seal of authenticity, of what is true and real. If there ever was a truly human being, an honorable man, this was he. His invitation to freedom is not an empty or demagogic statement; it is backed up by everything he ever said and did.

But, nonetheless, we still look for assurance that Jesus was more than an inspired and heroic dreamer. After all, his whole life was a struggle in which his message, his teachings, and his intentions were constantly being rejected, attacked, and denied not only by his enemies but by his followers as well. And finally he was crucified for his cause.

In this sense, the New Testament is harshly realistic. If

the cross is the last word, we are confronted with a magnificent example of humanity, but nothing more. Nothing universally and effectively backs up Jesus' life, and his followers are, as much as the words disgust us, "deceivers and deceived," or in the words of the apostle Paul "the unhappiest of men."

Where is our assurance? The seal of reality on Christ's life, according to the New Testament, is his resurrection. But the importance of the resurrection in the New Testament is not based on its astonishing or miraculous character. If God is truly God such a thing is not incredible at all. What is radically important is that in this act *God confirmed all that Jesus had been, said, and done.* It is for this reason that Paul explained that without the resurrection our faith has no foundation.

In religious terminology we say that Jesus documented with his life everything he taught us about the Creator, the God of love who wants to lift up humanity and place us on the road to a new world. With the resurrection God himself confirmed this documentation. There is no way to notarize this mysterious signature. The only thing we can do is present the check and see if we will collect on it. To gamble our own lives with *his* life as the guarantee. The New Testament is full of this kind of modern language. Paul even says that if the resurrection isn't true, if the confirmation is false, "God proves himself to be a liar." There is no other guarantee.

Challenge and Consolation

How do we come to trust in Christ, to put our faith in his life, his death, his resurrection? I think that we arrive at this in one of two ways: the way of *challenge* or the way of *consolation*.

There are those who are moved by the challenge of Jesus, by his plan for the liberation and transformation of humanity, by his call to a new kingdom. They perceive in this call the seal of what is real and true, and they respond enthusiastically and decisively: "I will follow you." With that decision, their lives take on meaning and value; they are given a mission which is at once universal and local, historical and eternal. Their new lives are dedicated. Even everyday events are seen as important elements of the one significant plan. The history of the church is full of people responding to this challenge. And today especially among the young, the prophetic message of the Bible and of Jesus evokes a generous and enthusiastic response.

Whoever accepts the challenge of Jesus, however, will soon find that the test is much greater than could ever have first been imagined. The invitation to change the world brings with it these challenging questions: "You who desire to transform the world, have you been transformed yourself? You who have committed yourself to bringing justice and love to the world, have you completely integrated this love and justice into your own motivations and attitudes, into your own values and actions? Are you really seeking the kingdom of God and the service of your neighbor, or are you only looking for a new kind of satisfaction and self-confirmation?"

It isn't a question of idealism. Even imperfect, subjective service is socially necessary and valuable. Christians need not transform themselves into introspective "perfectionists," constantly delving into their motivations, obsessed with the purity of their consciences. It is a question of understanding that once you dedicate yourself to a cause, a total commitment to it is required, and that the cause of human transformation is not something mechanical but exquisitely human. And therefore it demands an internal commitment. Whoever accepts the challenge of Jesus soon feels the need to fully dedicate himself or herself to that calling. They first perceive their own need for transformation and then,

together with Jesus, seek ever new dimensions in which to
fulfill all their needs.

In addition there are those who respond to the challenge
of Jesus when they are weary, failing, frustrated, faced with
problems that drain their inner strength. It may be that
they come to Jesus exhausted from a life-style that has de-
humanized them and left them feeling empty.

Many of us sometimes feel as though our lives are slowly
slipping through our fingers. We see the time allotted to us
as almost used up. We don't know what we have done with
it. And we do not know how to use the little time we have
left. Thus, the futility of our very lives drives us to Jesus.

Or perhaps the bad luck of loved ones whom we have
not been able to guide or help troubles us. Or our hearts
sicken because we have not been able to create a meaningful relationship with them. Maybe we are disturbed by
feelings of guilt and remorse for what we have done or
failed to do. A sense of blame or shame, whether real or
imagined, eats away at us. A feeling of impotence at cop-
ing with all kinds of problems inevitably leads us to seek
help, consolation, advice. And so we go to Jesus.

It All Begins with Forgiveness

I believe that people come to Jesus in one of two ways:
in response to the *challenge* or in search of *consolation*.
But both groups of individuals find a unique and personal
response. One fact is clear: in Jesus' eyes we are neither
pure heroes appointing ourselves as incorruptible champions
of the transformation of the world, nor are we innocent
victims who exist only to suffer for others. The right to be
consoled and strengthened in our need, or to be incorpo-
rated into the service of humanity and the world, is not
based on our perfection or imperfection. In order to get it,
we have to give ourselves over to it. To find Jesus is to find
a God who has no misgivings about the waverings in our

dedication, the lapses in our service, or the weakness in our actions. When he challenges us, "Follow me," he is also consoling us: "You are accepted as you are." When he tells us, "I will never cast out anyone who comes to me," he really means "There is no sin, blame, betrayal or infidelity which can ever shock me or separate me from you!"

When we look at the life of Jesus, we find at once an infinite severity in his denouncement of evil and an infinite tenderness in his acceptance of those who truly seek life. He didn't overlook the seriousness of the infidelity in those whom he met. No one got a "free pass" from Jesus. No one got a "special deal." On the other hand, never did he turn away anyone who came to him sincerely searching for truth. To find Jesus is not to meet someone who thinks about us from the heights of his own perfection: it is to find someone who takes part in our human condition, one who knows the joys and annoyances and frustrations and sorrows and indignations "which have been felt by all of us."

If we find the strength to overcome temptation, it is not from any infusion of abstract divinity but because of the love we feel for our fellow human beings. Jesus doesn't look at us arrogantly from the tower of his sanctity but from a humility grounded in love, often tempted but always victorious.

This then is the one who accepts us. And his acceptance is the triumph of love. Because if the true meaning of life is love, and if sin, selfishness, and hatred are its absence, then the only definitive response to life is that ultimate act of love which alone can overcome denial, frustration, betrayal, and infidelity.

There is no other way. What Jesus means, in the final analysis, is simply this, that God has told us through his whole way of being: "You have the right to be human beings; you can begin your duty; you are even partners with me in my plan for the making of the world; as you are and where you are, you are the beings on whom the Father relies and in whom he trusts. 'Get up and walk.' " These words reaffirm our society with him; they reestablish his initial plan for creation.

Challenge and consolation are two inseparable sides of the coin of faith. No one can really understand either one of them without being led to experience the other. Jesus Christ doesn't console us by persuading us that injustice, pain, blame, or evil don't exist, or by transporting us to some "spiritual plane" where these realities no longer bother us (as some priests frequently do). No, Jesus Christ consoles us by assuring us that these things don't have a future at all, that love has the last word, and that the world of justice and truth to which we aspire is the real future of all humanity. Therefore, true consolation produces an indestructible cry of protest, an inability to conform to the world as it is, a hopeful anxiety, a permanent concern for others. Faith permits us to put aside our own security, happiness, or poverty, but it does not permit us to put aside the need, poverty, insecurity, or pain of others.

It is true that this has not always been the attitude of the faithful or of the churches. One theologian spoke of the "cheapening of grace" for which we Christians are responsible. We have turned the message of the gospel into a cheap tranquilizer which allows us to misinterpret the challenge of the gospel. Therefore, it is essential, as we have said, to insist again on the true identity of Jesus Christ, of the God of the Bible who created the world and called us to join him. The forgiveness and consolation of this God are not drugs that will put us to sleep or transport us to a world of fantasy, but rather stimulants that rejuvenate us, make us get up and take up our human vocation again. Therefore, this God was not content to send down from his home a word of consolation; instead the Word became flesh, and descended, and made a home in our world to save us and teach us how to save ourselves from it while in it, and to launch the campaign for a new world and a new humankind.

Perhaps consolation and challenge are like the two openings in the same tunnel; you can enter through either one of them and if you keep on going you will eventually discover the other one. Challenge without consolation leads to desperation and frustration and, finally, destruction. Consolation without challenge brings with it spiritual death, the destruction of what is human. Only the hope which trusts and is practiced and has been affirmed by God belongs to the true faith.

The extraordinary thing about the gospel is that it invites us to come closer to Jesus Christ wherever we find ourselves: whether we are floating in some kind of euphoria and feel capable of taking the world in our own hands and remaking it, or if we are frozen in a state of anxiety and feel incapable of surviving the contradictions of life. No matter where we are, Christ will accept us as we are. However, we will probably always experience need and insufficiency from time to time and therefore we have to search for consolation and forgiveness, but we will sometimes experience the true euphoria as well, and know that we are on the road to the ultimate true reality.

THEMES FOR REFLECTION

Security and Risk

Jesus once said: "For whoever would save his life will lose it, and whoever loses his life for my sake and the gospel's will save it" (Mark 8:35). This statement has often been interpreted in terms of "two lives": one risks his life *here* and saves it *there*. We have already seen the inadequacy of this kind of thinking. According to the faith, there is only *one* life, the one which God lovingly gives us and invites us to live, the life which challenges and overcomes death. This passage really reflects Jesus' stance that those who let go of their own lives and risk themselves in the loving service of others will find the true origin and center of all life; they will be in contact with life as it really is both before and after death; they will live the true life.

This forces us to redefine "security" as applied to the Christian life. Since this security doesn't exclude risk, neither does it "protect" us from sickness, pain, frustration, or fear. The truth is, love *increases* these risks since no one is more vulnerable than the one who loves. There has never been anyone on this earth more vulnerable than Jesus. Or to put it another way, God is the most vulnerable being of all since he is open to everything that happens in the universe. Security, then, is not the elimination of risks, but the assurance of being in touch with what is true, or of being on firm ground. When Paul lists the things that can threaten us—persecution, danger, the attraction of things, the seductiveness of temptations, earthly or heavenly powers —he doesn't conclude that the Christian is exempt from these dangers but that "nothing can separate us from the love of God in Christ Jesus. . . ." This is the Christian concept of security. Perhaps Martin Luther clarified this best in his distinction between the words security and certainty. The Christian has the second but not the first.

The Mystery of the Good

"There are non-Christians who also accept the challenge and the consolation. But if Jesus Christ is the challenge and consolation for those who have the faith, where do those who do not have it get it?" We have already touched on this theme in chapter 1. But it would be helpful now to reflect a bit on it. We acknowledge that there are many individuals who do not profess to be Christians, or who specifically declare that they are atheists, but have nonetheless dedicated themselves entirely to God's plan for the transformation and humanization of the world and humanity through love. There are those who have given up all they cherish for it. And there are those who have done it and are doing it with great joy, generosity, and spiritual peace. Some non-Christians have felt this calling more clearly and have responded more decisively than some Christians. And many times, we Christians have experienced this response through the example and dedication of those who neither profess nor adhere to our faith.

We should, as we have said before, "acknowledge" that this is so. Yet this word is already suspect; it's as though we are reluctantly admitting that things are this way because we have no other choice. But such an attitude does not correspond to either the teaching or the attitude of the Bible. It is rather an expression of some kind of Christian imperialism, related more closely to the defense of the rights and privileges of the churches than to the gospel, a kind of pretense at their monopoly of good and virtue. On the other hand, according to the Bible, the Spirit of God is not confined within the walls of the church or inside the lines of the Creed. The Spirit of God is working throughout the entire world and in all men. God, as one biblical author has expressed it, "has not been left without witnesses." Paul has told us that "You have the law written on your conscience," and this law exposes our responsibility and stimulates our judgment. Therefore, it is not a matter of exalting these individuals' virtues since they, like ourselves, have sometimes failed in their response to this challenge of justice and good. However, God did not disappear from their lives either.

Is it not odd that we Christians get flustered when a non-Christian does or says anything that seems to us to correspond to the teaching of the Gospel? It seems as though we feel obligated to prove that the love and sacri-

fice and sensitivity that they practice are only fictitious
representations of our faith. However, in the Bible, when a
pagan performed a good deed, it was an occasion to praise
and thank God because his Spirit had acted powerfully in
the world, even among those who never acknowledged it.
The good which occurs outside our own religious orbit,
often in spite of or against what we ourselves do, should
also be an occasion for our praising God and for repenting.
It is in this way that God demonstrates the omnipresence
of his love and his fidelity to his plan.

However, all of this doesn't mean that we Christians
should conceal or be quiet about the fact that the most profound responses by non-Christians to the challenge and
consolation can come only from Jesus Christ himself. This
response, first and fully in Jesus, is neither a frail human
disposition nor a voluntary heroic commitment but rather
the most profound basis for creation and the true meaning
of history and the universe. It is the ultimate secret of
reality and appears in Jesus as the very being of God.
Therefore, only in the knowledge of Jesus Christ can the
depth of the challenge and the fullness of the consolation
be perceived. In this sense, we Christians have neither the
monopoly on the understanding nor the fulfillment of this
response. We only know where the source of all true
challenge and effective consolation and all searching for
justice and love is. For this reason we should be concerned
with our responsibility to bear witness to this knowledge.
At the same time, the credibility of our witness is indis-
solubly tied to the fidelity of our response.

Consolation without Challenge

A minimum measure of objectivity and honesty obliges
us to acknowledge that we do not often find in our churches
the kind of faith which is dedicated to the transformation
of the world through justice and love. What we too often

find in our churches are people "comfortably installed" there, feeling complacent about who they think they are and practicing their religion for their own benefit, people who at best perform isolated acts of "charity," and who are more determined to salve their own consciences than to transform reality or effectively and permanently serve their neighbor.

It would be beneficial to look at this problem from several different points of view. First we should ask ourselves: Who are the Christians? During the fourth and fifth centuries, the church became part of the Roman Empire. The Christian religion was passed on later to other Western cultures until it finally became the faith of everyone in the Western world. However, when everyone professes Christianity we have difficulty determining who the real Christians are. Does the faith then become merely a generic designation for a whole culture, or is it still an active commitment? When an entire country becomes Christian, the uniqueness of the faith gets lost. The God revealed by Jesus becomes confused with the gods who are merely symbols of the nation. It is not strange then that under these conditions the faith becomes a "bland consolation" rather that a challenge.

Our second observation, which is of a more sociological nature, concerns the churches that were founded by that sector of society usually referred to as the "middle class." Here in Argentina, this group would include most of the Protestant faiths and the more ecclesiastically active Catholic groups. In any event, it would certainly include those who most often attend religious services (and those who would probably read this book). The faith of this group is unfortunately characterized by two traits—subjectivity and individualism. They live for themselves, introvertedly, dreaming of their own houses, their own vacations, their own privacy. And their religion has these same characteristics. Since they do not share their lives, they do not share their faith.

We dare not risk exposing ourselves by revealing our personal intimacy or abandoning our privacy. The world is presented as an enemy territory from which we have to take away those things which contribute to our personal happiness and enjoy them in our own little world with "our own" —family, friends, or even religious congregation. This sociological determination inhibits us from seeing the greater world of society, politics, the economy, and even the material, structural world like our home, the place we call our own, the world of God.

This attitude creates a vacuum, especially in the theological or religious aspects of our lives. If these wider areas of human life are foreign to us, we have not applied the message of the Bible. We have not asked ourselves seriously and urgently what meaning our faith can have in the areas of politics or the economy, not as mere speculation but as understanding and practice. That is why we need a specific witness or practice which would identify us as Christians. We are lacking the community awareness which could create Christian witness.

At certain decisive moments in their history, our churches have demonstrated these specific traits. There can be no mistake about how a Christian community could be founded and survive in Imperial Rome during the first and second centuries, or what it meant to become part of the "Methodist community" in eighteenth-century England. We can either agree with these militant Christian congregations or not. However, they were, in any case, representative of a concrete manifestation of the message in historical situations and specific community practices. Without them we would still be viewing our religions in terms of private consolation rather than historical challenge.

These observations raise the question of conversion. In

effect, the birth of a community of faith and practice—of a concrete Christian militancy—and the beginnings of a universal Christianity would demand of a personal religion the awakening of one's personal conscience and presume a commitment. It would involve a radical revision of our religion; in short, it would demand the qualitative jump which we call "conversion." Therefore, it is imperative that we recover the biblical message as identified in the person of Jesus, because only the rediscovery of the identity of God himself can call for the transformation of the world and can produce an acceptance in us radical enough to effect a conversion.

A religion of consolation without challenge is, then, a distortion of the faith. A true conversion must emerge from it, one which can transform our understanding and practice. This conversion must manifest itself in our time first through our recognition of the call to a historical militancy and then to our participation in the construction of a new world and a new humankind. And it is this very dimension of our life that has been neutralized by our subjective and private religion.

It would be a mistake to call this conversion a voluntary and ethical response to the plan for the transformation of society. A challenge without the profound depths of forgiveness and consolation is merely a mirage. It can only lead to frustration and disillusionment, while the true challenge leads us to recognize the danger of material gain, the infidelities of our dedication, and the deficiencies of the groups and projects in which we have become involved. Only when we incorporate militancy into the universal plan of divine love, will we be able to maintain our integrity without giving up the fight.

At the same time, the true challenge is purely voluntary, asking us to overcome any temptation to arrogance or self-justification so that the dignity of the cause never gets confused with our own identity. In that case we would demand for ourselves an infallibility, an obedience, an honor which only the cause itself merits. Arrogance leads people to hide their imperfections from others and even themselves.

Those who have accepted the call of Christ no longer have to defend their own dignity, no longer have any status to protect. And therefore, they can dedicate themselves freely and humbly to their duty without proclaiming their own virtues and without becoming discouraged if ever they get lost along the way to the new world. Consolation and challenge are the two inseparable dimensions of a faith which moves through love.